God's promises® for girls

jack countryman & amy parker

Illustrations by Rachelle Miller

A Division of Thomas Nelson Publishers

NASHVILLE   DALLAS   MEXICO CITY   RIO DE JANEIRO

Contents

God's Promises for You

You Live Like His Princess

Did you know you're a princess?
Yes, a daughter of the King!
So live the life of royalty,
And show the joy God's love can bring!

Trust the Lord and do good.
Live in the land and enjoy its safety.
Enjoy serving the Lord.
And he will give you what you want.
Depend on the Lord.
Trust him, and he will take care of you.
Then your goodness will shine like the sun.
Your fairness will shine like the noonday sun.

PSALM 37:3–6

• • •

You are children of the Lord your God. . . .
He has chosen you from all the people on
earth to be his very own.

DEUTERONOMY 14:1–2

It is not fancy hair, gold jewelry, or fine clothes that should make you beautiful. No, your beauty should come from within you—the beauty of a gentle and quiet spirit. This beauty will never disappear, and it is worth very much to God.

1 PETER 3:3—4

You Are Happy

Hooray! It's a wonderful day!
Picking daisies is oh, so fun . . .
There is always a reason to be happy,
When you're living for Jesus the Son!

Ask and you will receive.
And your joy will be the fullest joy.

JOHN 16:24

• • •

You have not seen Christ, but still you love him.
You cannot see him now, but you believe in him.
You are filled with a joy that cannot be explained.
And that joy is full of glory.

1 PETER 1:8

• • •

The Lord makes me very happy.
All that I am rejoices in my God.
The Lord has covered me with clothes of salvation.
He has covered me with a coat of goodness.

ISAIAH 61:10

• • •

The Lord has done great things for us,
and we are very glad.

PSALM 126:3

You Are Thankful

For parents and friends who love you,
For a cuddly doll to hold tight,
For the earth, the sky, and the sea—
Say, "Thank You, God!" with all your might.

Thanks be to God for his gift that is too
wonderful to explain.

2 CORINTHIANS 9:15

Thank the Lord because he is good.
His love continues forever.

1 CHRONICLES 16:34

The Lord is my strength and shield.
I trust him, and he helps me.
I am very happy.
And I praise him with my song.

PSALM 28:7

Come, let's bow down and worship him.
Let's kneel before the Lord who made us.
He is our God.
And we are the people he takes care of
and the sheep that he tends.

PSALM 95:6–7

You Are Worried

Dear, precious one, don't you worry;
Sweet, little girl, don't you fret!
God hasn't met *any* problem
That's been too big for Him yet!

Give your worries to the Lord.
He will take care of you.

PSALM 55:22

• • •

You, Lord, give true peace.
You give peace to those who depend on you.
You give peace to those who trust you.
So, trust the Lord always.
Trust the Lord because he is our Rock forever.

ISAIAH 26:3—4

• • •

"I leave you peace. My peace I give you. I do not give
it to you as the world does. So don't let your hearts
be troubled. Don't be afraid."

JOHN 14:27

• • •

So be humble under God's powerful hand. Then he
will lift you up when the right time comes. Give all
your worries to him, because he cares for you.

1 PETER 5:6—7

You Need Help

Searching for help? Nowhere to turn?
You've looked both high and low?
There's just one thing to remember:
Prayer is the best place to go.

People, trust God all the time.
Tell him all your problems.
God is our protection.

PSALM 62:8

Trust the Lord with all your heart.
Don't depend on your own understanding.
Remember the Lord in everything you do.
And he will give you success.

PROVERBS 3:5—6

So our hope is in the Lord.
He is our help, our shield to protect us.

PSALM 33:20

God is our protection and our strength.
He always helps in times of trouble.
So we will not be afraid if the earth shakes,
or if the mountains fall into the sea.

PSALM 46:1—2

You Feel Guilty

When you've lost your mom's best bracelet
Or you've made your best friend feel bad,
"I'm sorry" are the magic words
That will help turn sad into glad!

"God did not send his Son into the world to judge the world guilty, but to save the world through him. He who believes in God's Son is not judged guilty."

JOHN 3:17–18

. . .

If anyone belongs to Christ, then he is made new. The old things have gone; everything is made new!

2 CORINTHIANS 5:17

. . .

"I tell you the truth. Whoever hears what I say and believes in the One who sent me has eternal life. He will not be judged guilty. He has already left death and has entered into life."

JOHN 5:24

. . .

"Don't judge other people, and you will not be judged. Don't accuse others of being guilty, and you will not be accused of being guilty. Forgive other people, and you will be forgiven."

LUKE 6:37

You Are Tempted to Do the Wrong Thing

The smell of fresh cookies fills the air,
But you remember Mom saying, "Don't!"
So when a sneaky voice says, "Yes, you *can*,"
Make sure your reply is, "I won't!"

[Y]ou can trust God. He will not let you be tempted more than you can stand. But when you are tempted, God will also give you a way to escape that temptation. Then you will be able to stand it.

1 CORINTHIANS 10:13

· · ·

Control yourselves and be careful! The devil is your enemy. And he goes around like a roaring lion looking for someone to eat. Refuse to give in to the devil. Stand strong in your faith.

1 PETER 5:8—9

For this reason Jesus had to be made like his brothers
in every way. . . . And now he can help those who
are tempted. He is able to help because he
himself suffered and was tempted.

HEBREWS 2:17–18

You Feel Lonely

Feeling left out and a little sad?
Stuck in the lonely zone?
Go to the One who is *always* there,
And you'll never be alone.

So don't worry, because I am with you.
Don't be afraid, because I am your God.
I will make you strong and will help you.
I will support you with my right hand that saves you.

ISAIAH 41:10

. . .

"The mountains may disappear,
and the hills may come to an end.
But my love will never disappear.
My promise of peace will not come to an end,"
says the Lord who shows mercy to you.

ISAIAH 54:10

. . .

"I am with you and I will save you," says the Lord.

JEREMIAH 30:11

. . .

"You can be sure that I will be with you always. I will
continue with you until the end of the world."

MATTHEW 28:20

You Need Comfort

When your very best friend moves away
Or your dolly can't be found,
Turn to God, and you will find
His comforting love all around.

Praise be to the God and Father of our Lord Jesus
Christ. God is the Father who is full of mercy.
And he is the God of all comfort. He comforts us every
time we have trouble, so that we can comfort others
when they have trouble. We can comfort them with
the same comfort that God gives us.

2 CORINTHIANS 1:3–4

· · ·

The Lord says, "I am the one who comforts you."

ISAIAH 51:12

· · ·

God comforts those who are troubled.

2 CORINTHIANS 7:6

Jesus said, "Don't let your hearts be troubled.
Trust in God. And trust in me."

JOHN 14:1

You Need Forgiveness

After you've said, "I'm sorry,"
God will take care of the rest.
He'll forget those bad things you've done
And only remember the best!

He has not punished us as our sins should be punished.
He has not repaid us for the evil we have done. . . .
He has taken our sins away from us
as far as the east is from west.

PSALM 103:10, 12

. . .

The Lord forgives me for all my sins.
He heals all my diseases.
He saves my life from the grave.
He loads me with love and mercy.

PSALM 103:3–4

. . .

Happy is the person whose sins are forgiven,
whose wrongs are pardoned.
Happy is the person
whom the Lord does not consider guilty.
In that person there is nothing false.

PSALM 32:1–2

. . .

If we confess our sins, he will forgive our sins.

1 JOHN 1:9

You Are Angry

Did that girl in your class tattle on you?
Did your brother ruin your art?
Don't yell; don't pout; don't go around mad;
Ask God to put peace in your heart.

Always be willing to listen and slow to speak. Do not become angry easily. Anger will not help you live a good life as God wants. So put out of your life every evil thing and every kind of wrong you do. Don't be proud but accept God's teaching that is planted in your hearts. This teaching can save your souls.

JAMES 1:19–21

. . .

A gentle answer will calm a person's anger.
But an unkind answer will cause more anger.

PROVERBS 15:1

Do not be angry with each other, but forgive each other. If someone does wrong to you, then forgive him. Forgive each other because the Lord forgave you.

COLOSSIANS 3:13

You Want Your Own Way

When you really want to play dress-up,
But your friends all want to play dolls,
Don't demand your own way—just keep your cool!
Then choose what works best for you *all*!

A wise person is careful and stays out of trouble.
But a foolish person is quick to act and careless.
A person who quickly loses his temper
does foolish things.
But a person with understanding remains calm.

PROVERBS 14:16—17

. . .

Yes, God is working in you to help you want
to do what pleases him. Then he gives you
the power to do it.

PHILIPPIANS 2:13

. . .

Help me obey your commands
because that makes me happy.
Help me want to obey your rules
instead of selfishly wanting riches.

PSALM 119:35—36

You Are Afraid

Monsters. Spiders. Being alone.
Do these things make you tremble in fear?
When you're afraid, remember these words:
God is with you; He's always near!

God did not give us a spirit that makes us afraid. He gave
us a spirit of power and love and self-control.

2 TIMOTHY 1:7

• • •

The Spirit that we received is not a spirit that makes us
slaves again to fear. The Spirit that we have makes us
children of God. And with that Spirit we say,
"Father, dear Father." And the Spirit himself joins
with our spirits to say that we are God's children.
If we are God's children, then we will receive the
blessings God has for us.

ROMANS 8:15—17

Where God's love is, there is no fear, because
God's perfect love takes away fear.

1 JOHN 4:18

. . .

I will not be afraid because the Lord is with me.
People can't do anything to me.

PSALM 118:6

The Woman You'll Grow Up to Be

Noble and gentle, loving and kind,
More valuable than rubies . . .
Stay faithful and true, then one day you'll find,
You're the woman God wants you to be!

"I am the true vine; my Father is the gardener. . . .
Remain in me, and I will remain in you. No branch
can produce fruit alone. It must remain in the vine. It
is the same with you. You cannot produce fruit alone.
You must remain in me."

JOHN 15:1, 4

. . .

God has chosen you and made you his holy people. He
loves you. So always do these things: Show mercy to
others; be kind, humble, gentle, and patient.

COLOSSIANS 3:12

. . .

"You are the light that gives light to the world. A city
that is built on a hill cannot be hidden. And people
don't hide a light under a bowl. They put the light
on a lampstand. Then the light shines for all the
people in the house. In the same way, you should be
a light for other people. Live so that they will
see the good things you do. Live so that they will
praise your Father in heaven."

MATTHEW 5:14—16

God's Love

Is God's love deep in your heart?
It's time to let it show!
Share a smile! Give a hug!
Let it overflow!

This is how God showed his love to us: He sent his only Son into the world to give us life through him. True love is God's love for us, not our love for God. God sent his Son to die in our place to take away our sins.

1 JOHN 4:9–10

• • •

But if someone obeys God's teaching, then God's love has truly arrived at its goal in him.

1 JOHN 2:5

And this hope will never disappoint us,
because God has poured out his love to fill our hearts.
God gave us his love through the Holy Spirit,
whom God has given to us.

ROMANS 5:5

• • •

But dear friends, use your most holy faith to build yourselves up strong. Pray with the Holy Spirit. Keep yourselves in God's love. Wait for the Lord Jesus Christ with his mercy to give you life forever.

JUDE 20–21

God's Grace

It's a second chance when you mess up,
Or God going easy when He could be tough.
When you ask, He will always forgive.
Yes, God's grace is more than enough.

The Word was full of grace and truth. From him we
all received more and more blessings.

JOHN 1:16

· · ·

And before the world was made, God decided to
make us his own children through Jesus Christ.
That was what he wanted and what pleased him.
This brings praise to God because of his wonderful
grace. God gave that grace to us freely, in Christ,
the One he loves. In Christ we are set free by the
blood of his death. And so we have forgiveness
of sins because of God's rich grace.

EPHESIANS 1:5–7

The Lord God is like our sun and shield.
The Lord gives us kindness and glory.
He does not hold back anything good
from those whose life is innocent.

PSALM 84:11

God's Gift of the Holy Spirit

Listen closely to the Holy Spirit. . . .
With your heart you'll understand:
It's the feeling that tells you
what's right and true;
It's God's own helping hand.

40

"But the Helper will teach you everything. He will cause you to remember all the things I told you. This Helper is the Holy Spirit whom the Father will send in my name."

JOHN 14:26

. . .

Jesus said to them, . . . "[T]he Holy Spirit will come to you. Then you will receive power. You will be my witnesses—in Jerusalem, in all of Judea, in Samaria, and in every part of the world."

ACTS 1:7–8

. . .

But when the Spirit of truth comes he will lead you into all truth. He will not speak his own words. He will speak only what he hears and will tell you what is to come. The Spirit of truth will bring glory to me. He will take what I have to say and tell it to you. All that the Father has is mine. That is why I said that the Spirit will take what I have to say and tell it to you.

JOHN 16:13–15

Praising God

Sing a song! Clap your hands!
You can even dance a jig!
Praise God's name for all He's done,
And be sure to do it BIG!

Happy are the people who know how to praise you.
Lord, let them live in the light of your presence.

PSALM 89:15

"God is the one who saves me.
I trust him. I am not afraid.
The Lord, the Lord, gives me strength and makes me sing.
He has saved me."

ISAIAH 12:2

I praise the Lord because he does what is right.
I sing praises to the name of the Lord Most High.

PSALM 7:17

I will always sing about the Lord's love.
I will tell of his loyalty from now on.
I will say, "Your love continues forever.
Your loyalty goes on and on like the sky."

PSALM 89:1—2

Obeying Your Parents

A hug, a kiss, a "please," and a "thank you,"
A "yes, ma'am" and a "yes, sir"—
In all these ways you obey God's command
To honor your mother and father.

"Honor your father and your mother.
Then you will live a long time in the land."

EXODUS 20:12

. • .

[K]eep your father's commands.
Don't forget your mother's teaching.
Remember their words forever.
Let it be as if they were tied around your neck.
They will guide you when you walk.
They will guard you while you sleep.
They will speak to you when you are awake.

PROVERBS 6:20—22

. • .

Children, obey your parents the way the Lord wants.
This is the right thing to do. The command says,
"Honor your father and mother." This is the first
command that has a promise with it. The promise is:
"Then everything will be well with you, and you will
have a long life on the earth."

EPHESIANS 6:1—3

Being a Good Sister

Even when Brother eats the last brownie,
Or when Sister hogs the TV,
Always remember how important it is
To be the sister *God* wants you to be.

"My true brother and sister and mother are those
who do the things God wants."

MARK 3:35

• • •

Do everything without complaining or arguing. Then
you will be innocent and without anything wrong in
you. You will be God's children without fault.

PHILIPPIANS 2:14—15

• • •

Most importantly, love each other deeply. Love has
a way of not looking at others' sins.

1 PETER 4:8

[L]ove each other. Love is what holds you all
together in perfect unity.

COLOSSIANS 3:14

Loving Others

Be a good friend; be caring and kind;
Love others as Jesus loves you.
There's no greater way to show others Christ
Than to love as He asks you to.

"I loved you as the Father loved me. Now remain in my love. I have obeyed my Father's commands, and I remain in his love. . . . I have told you these things so that you can have the same joy I have. I want your joy to be the fullest joy."

JOHN 15:9–11

. • •

"I give you a new command: Love each other. You must love each other as I have loved you. All people will know that you are my followers if you love each other."

JOHN 13:34–35

. • •

Now you have made yourselves pure by obeying the truth. Now you can have true love for your brothers. So love each other deeply with all your heart.

1 PETER 1:22

. • •

We love because God first loved us.

1 JOHN 4:19

Being a Good Daughter

She's courteous, helpful, and kind;
She serves her family in love.
She's honest, pure, and polite—
A daughter to be proud of!

It always gives me the greatest joy when I hear that
my children are following the way of truth.

3 JOHN 4

• • •

How can a young person live a pure life?
He can do it by obeying your word.

PSALM 119:9

• • •

Always remember what you have been taught.
Don't let go of it. Keep safe all that you have learned.
It is the most important thing in your life.

PROVERBS 4:13

Don't ever stop being kind and truthful.
Let kindness and truth show in all you do.
Write them down in your mind as if on a tablet.
Then you will be respected
and pleasing to both God and men.

PROVERBS 3:3–4

Being Kind and Good

Pick a daisy for Mom, make brownies for Dad,
And act as you know you should. . . .
Now look around for many more ways
That you can be kind and good.

Be kind and loving to each other. Forgive each other just as God forgave you in Christ.

EPHESIANS 4:32

. . .

Love is patient and kind. Love is not jealous, it does not brag, and it is not proud. Love is not rude, is not selfish, and does not become angry easily. Love does not remember wrongs done against it. Love takes no pleasure in evil, but rejoices over the truth. Love patiently accepts all things. It always trusts, always hopes, and always continues strong.

1 CORINTHIANS 13:4–7

. . .

So love your enemies. Do good to them, and lend to them without hoping to get anything back. If you do these things, you will have a great reward.

LUKE 6:35

. . .

Being kind to the poor is like lending to the Lord. The Lord will reward you for what you have done.

PROVERBS 19:17

Praying for Your Family

Brothers, sisters, uncles, and aunts,
Grandmommies and granddaddies too—
Pray a prayer for your family,
And thank God for giving them to you!

"I will look to the Lord for help.
I will wait for God to save me.
My God will hear me."

MICAH 7:7

• • •

You will find pleasure in God All-Powerful.
And you will look up to him.
You will pray to him, and he will hear you.
And you will keep your promises to him.

JOB 22:26—27

"God has heard your prayers. . . . And God remembers you."

Acts 10:4

. . .

[T]he Lord is faithful. . . . We pray that the Lord will lead your hearts into God's love and Christ's patience.

2 Thessalonians 3:3, 5

Being a Better Friend

Grouchy, selfish, and cutting in line—
What kind of friend will you be?
Caring and sharing, loving and kind—
Sounds like a great friend to me!

"Whoever helps one of these little ones because they are my followers will truly get his reward. He will get his reward even if he only gave my follower a cup of cold water."

MATTHEW 10:42

· · ·

"[N]ow I call you friends because I have made known to you everything I heard from my Father. You did not choose me; I chose you. And I gave you this work, to go and produce fruit. I want you to produce fruit that will last. Then the Father will give you anything you ask for in my name."

JOHN 15:15—16

· · ·

Two people are better than one.
They get more done by working together.
If one person falls, the other can help him up.
But it is bad for the person who is alone when he falls.
No one is there to help him.

ECCLESIASTES 4:9—10

Praying for Others

When someone's hurting or being mean,
Take a moment to send up a prayer.
It's God's promise that if you just ask,
His answers will always be there.

First, I tell you to pray for all people. Ask God for the things people need, and be thankful to him. You should pray for kings and for all who have authority. Pray for the leaders so that we can have quiet and peaceful lives—lives full of worship and respect for God.

1 TIMOTHY 2:1–2

• • •

Confess your sins to each other and pray for each other. Do this so that God can heal you. When a good man prays, great things happen.

JAMES 5:16

"Also, I tell you that if two of you on earth agree about something, then you can pray for it. And the thing you ask for will be done for you by my Father in heaven. This is true because if two or three people come together in my name, I am there with them."

MATTHEW 18:19—20

Serving Others

Share a doll, show the new girl around,
Bake brownies and take them next door;
Serving and helping others in love
Is what God created you for!

Serve the Lord with joy.
Come before him with singing.
Know that the Lord is God.
He made us, and we belong to him.
We are his people, the sheep he tends.

PSALM 100:2–3

. . .

There might be a poor man among you. He might be in one of the towns of the land the Lord your God is giving you. Do not be selfish or greedy toward your poor brother. But give freely to him. Freely lend him whatever he needs. . . . The Lord your God will bless your work and everything you touch.

DEUTERONOMY 15:7–8, 10

. . .

Religion that God the Father accepts is this: caring for orphans or widows who need help; and keeping yourself free from the world's evil influence. This is the kind of religion that God accepts as pure and good.

JAMES 1:27

Being a Christian

Do your friends know you're a Christian?
Can they tell by what you *do* and *say*?
Shout the Good News! Do what is right!
Be a Christian in every way!

Jesus said to the followers, "Go everywhere in the world. Tell the Good News to everyone." . . . The followers went everywhere in the world and told the Good News to people. And the Lord helped them.

MARK 16:15, 20

· · ·

"If anyone stands before other people and says he believes in me, then I will say that he belongs to me. I will say this before my Father in heaven."

MATTHEW 10:32

When God makes someone his child, that person does not go on sinning. The new life God gave that person stays in him. So he is not able to go on sinning, because he has become a child of God.

1 JOHN 3:9

Use Your Time Wisely

You were put here for a reason—
There's a job God wants *you* to do!
Use *every* moment of every day
To fulfill God's purpose in you!

The lazy person will not get what he wants.
But a hard worker gets everything he wants.

PROVERBS 13:4

· · ·

Hard workers will become leaders.

PROVERBS 12:24

· · ·

Depend on the Lord in whatever you do.
Then your plans will succeed.

PROVERBS 16:3

· · ·

People who live good lives show respect for the Lord.
But those who live evil lives show no respect for him.

PROVERBS 14:2

· · ·

There is a right time for everything.
Everything on earth has its special season.

ECCLESIASTES 3:1

Please Him

Think about your actions . . .
The things you say and do . . .
Are you pleasing the Lord?
Or are you pleasing you?

"The time is coming when the true worshipers will
worship the Father in spirit and truth. That time is
now here. And these are the kinds of worshipers the
Father wants. God is spirit. Those who worship God
must worship in spirit and truth."

JOHN 4:23–24

· · ·

[Y]ou will live the kind of life that honors and pleases
the Lord in every way. You will produce fruit in every
good work and grow in the knowledge of God.

COLOSSIANS 1:10

"Love the Lord your God. Love him with all your heart, all your soul, all your strength, and all your mind." Also, "You must love your neighbor as you love yourself."
Jesus said to him, "Your answer is right. Do this and you will have life forever."

Learn More about Him

A love truer than Prince Charming's,
A story better than a fairy tale—
Read all about your King, your God,
Who loves and knows *you* well.

You were bought with the precious blood of the death of Christ, who was like a pure and perfect lamb. Christ was chosen before the world was made. But he was shown to the world in these last times for you. You believe in God through Christ. God raised Christ from death and gave him glory. So your faith and your hope are in God.

1 PETER 1:19–21

* * *

You have been born again. This new life did not come from something that dies, but from something that cannot die. You were born again through God's living message that continues forever.

1 PETER 1:23

* * *

So be careful. Do not let those evil people lead you away by the wrong they do. Be careful so that you will not fall from your own strong faith. But grow in the grace and knowledge of our Lord and Savior Jesus Christ. Glory be to him now and forever! Amen.

2 PETER 3:17–18

Keep Dancing!

No matter the weather, sunny or gray,
Whether you're happy or sad,
There's *always* a way to find joy in the Lord,
So keep dancing! Rejoice and be glad!

And from far away the Lord appeared to his people. He said,
"I love you people with a love that will last forever.
I became your friend because of my love and kindness.
People of Israel, I will build you up again, and you
will be rebuilt.
You will pick up your tambourines again.
You will dance with those who are joyful."

JEREMIAH 31:3–4

• • •

They should praise him with dancing.
They should praise him with tambourines and harps.
The Lord is pleased with his people.
He saves those who are not proud.

PSALM 149:3–4

You changed my sorrow into dancing.
You took away my rough cloth, which shows sadness,
and clothed me in happiness.
I will sing to you and not be silent.
Lord, my God, I will praise you forever.

PSALM 30:11–12

Count Your Blessings

One is for my Father in heaven;
Two is for my mom and my dad;
Three is for my two brothers and *me*!
And *every day* I have blessings to add!

Every good action and every perfect gift is from God. These good gifts come down from the Creator of the sun, moon, and stars. . . . He wanted us to be the most important of all the things he made.

JAMES 1:17—18

• • •

God is the One who gives seed to the farmer. And he gives bread for food. And God will give you all the seed you need and make it grow. He will make a great harvest from your goodness. God will make you rich in every way so that you can always give freely. And your giving through us will cause many to give thanks to God.

2 CORINTHIANS 9:10—11

• • •

Praise be to the God and Father of our Lord Jesus Christ. In Christ, God has given us every spiritual blessing in heaven. In Christ, he chose us before the world was made. In his love he chose us to be his holy people—people without blame before him.

EPHESIANS 1:3—4

Share with Others

What gift can you give?
What talents can you share?
Use your time and talents—
Show God's love everywhere!

Let us hold firmly to the hope that we have
confessed. We can trust God to do what he promised.
Let us think about each other and help each other
to show love and do good deeds.

HEBREWS 10:23–24

· · ·

"Give, and you will receive. You will be given much.
It will be poured into your hands—more than you
can hold. You will be given so much that it will
spill into your lap. The way you give to others
is the way God will give to you."

LUKE 6:38

And Christ gave gifts to men—he made some to be apostles, some to be prophets, some to go and tell the Good News, and some to have the work of caring for and teaching God's people. Christ gave those gifts to prepare God's holy people for the work of serving. He gave those gifts to make the body of Christ stronger.

EPHESIANS 4:11-12

Tell the Truth

White lies, fibs, or stretching the truth—
Dishonesty makes God sad.
He wants you to be honest;
Tell the truth and make Him glad.

Do not lie to each other. You have left your old sinful life and the things you did before. You have begun to live the new life. In your new life you are being made new. You are becoming like the One who made you. This new life brings you the true knowledge of God.

COLOSSIANS 3:9—10

. . .

Lord, who may enter your Holy Tent?
Who may live on your holy mountain?
Only a person who is innocent
and who does what is right.
He must speak the truth from his heart.
He must not tell lies about others.
He must do no wrong to his neighbors.
He must not gossip.

PSALM 15:1—3

. . .

A light shines in the dark for honest people.
It shines for those who are good and
kind and merciful.

PSALM 112:4

Be a Good Sport

The referee blew his whistle in your face,
And the other team just stole the ball. . . .
Yet making sure you have a good attitude
Is the winning-est rule of them all.

This is my prayer for you: that your love will grow more and more; that you will have knowledge and understanding with your love; that you will see the difference between good and bad and choose the good; that you will be pure and without wrong for the coming of Christ; that you will be filled with the good things produced in your life by Christ to bring glory and praise to God.

PHILIPPIANS 1:9–11

. . .

You should do good deeds to be an example in every way. . . . That is the way we should live, because God's grace has come. That grace can save every person.

TITUS 2:7, 11

. . .

Dear friends, we should love each other, because love comes from God. The person who loves has become God's child and knows God. Whoever does not love does not know God, because God is love.

1 JOHN 4:7–8

Be Beautiful on the Inside

Lip gloss and nail polish,
Fancy clothes and earrings—
None of these compare with
What inner beauty brings.

She is strong and is respected by the people.
She looks forward to the future with joy.
She speaks wise words.
And she teaches others to be kind.
She watches over her family.
And she is always busy.
Her children bless her.
Her husband also praises her.
He says, "There are many excellent wives,
but you are better than all of them."
Charm can fool you, and beauty can trick you.
But a woman who respects the Lord should be praised.

PROVERBS 31:25—30

"God does not see the same way people see.
People look at the outside of a person,
but the Lord looks at the heart."

1 SAMUEL 16:7

You Don't Feel Important

When you feel you're not good enough,
Remember how GREAT your God is!
He made *everyone* in this world—
You know what that means?! You are *HIS*!

And I pray that you and all God's holy people will have the power to understand the greatness of Christ's love. I pray that you can understand how wide and how long and how high and how deep that love is. Christ's love is greater than any person can ever know. But I pray that you will be able to know that love. Then you can be filled with the fullness of God.

EPHESIANS 3:18–19

. . .

I can do all things through Christ because he gives me strength.

PHILIPPIANS 4:13

. . .

God began doing a good work in you. And he will continue it until it is finished when Jesus Christ comes again. I am sure of that.

PHILIPPIANS 1:6

You Find Yourself in Trouble

Let me tell you a secret:
We *all* stumble along the way.
When you mess up, take it to God,
And He will make it okay.

We have troubles all around us, but we are not
defeated. We do not know what to do, but we do not
give up. We are persecuted, but God does not leave us.
We are hurt sometimes, but we are not destroyed.

2 CORINTHIANS 4:8–9

• • •

The Lord is good.
He gives protection in times of trouble.
He knows who trusts in him.

NAHUM 1:7

Now this is what the Lord says. . . .
"Don't be afraid, because I have saved you."

ISAIAH 43:1

• • •

Do not worry about anything. But pray and ask God
for everything you need. And when you pray, always
give thanks. And God's peace will keep your hearts and
minds in Christ Jesus. The peace that God gives is so
great that we cannot understand it.

PHILIPPIANS 4:6–7

You Are Sick

Do you think you'll *never* get better?
Are you icky, sicky, or blue?
Just rest, relax, and remember
God's promise of healing for you.

If one of you is sick, he should call the church's elders.
The elders should pour oil on him in the name of the
Lord and pray for him. And the prayer that is said with
faith will make the sick person well. The Lord will heal
him. And if he has sinned, God will forgive him.

JAMES 5:14—15

. . .

My child, pay attention to my words.
Listen closely to what I say.
Don't ever forget my words.
Keep them deep within your heart.
These words are the secret to life for those who find them.
They bring health to the whole body.

PROVERBS 4:20—22

. . .

"I am the Lord. I am the Lord who heals you."

EXODUS 15:26

. . .

Lord, heal me, and I will truly be healed.
Save me, and I will truly be saved.
Lord, you are the one I praise.

JEREMIAH 17:14

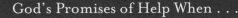

Nothing Is Going Right

A fight with your friend and big, frizzy hair—
Nothing is going right!
But even when all around you goes wrong,
Live like a child of the light!

We know that in everything God works for
the good of those who love him.

ROMANS 8:28

. . .

[L]ive like children who belong
to the light. Light brings every kind of goodness,
right living, and truth.

EPHESIANS 5:8–9

. . .

The ways of God are without fault. The Lord's words
are pure. He is a shield to those who trust him.

PSALM 18:30

Sing praises to the Lord, you who belong to him.
Praise his holy name.
His anger lasts only a moment.
But his kindness lasts for a lifetime.
Crying may last for a night.
But joy comes in the morning.

PSALM 30:4—5

Growing Up Is Hard

Yes, growing up can be tough—
Just ask your mom or your dad.
But know that God walks with you.
Through the good times and the bad!

As newborn babies want milk, you should want
the pure and simple teaching. By it you can
mature in your salvation.

1 PETER 2:2

. . .

Jesus will keep you strong until the end. He will keep
you strong, so that there will be no wrong in you on
the day our Lord Jesus Christ comes again. God is
faithful. He is the One who has called you to share life
with his Son, Jesus Christ our Lord.

1 CORINTHIANS 1:8–9

. . .

My friends, do not be surprised at the painful things
you are now suffering. These things are testing your
faith. So do not think that something strange is
happening to you. But you should be happy that you
are sharing in Christ's sufferings. You will be happy
and full of joy when Christ comes again in glory.

1 PETER 4:12–13

You Need Patience

Waiting for what you want . . .
Wanting while you wait . . .
It's never easy to be patient,
But the rewards are always great!

Let your patience show itself perfectly in what
you do. Then you will be perfect and complete.
You will have everything you need.

JAMES 1:4

Wait for the Lord's help.
Be strong and brave
and wait for the Lord's help.

PSALM 27:14

The Lord is good to those who put their hope in him.
He is good to those who look to him for help.
It is good to wait quietly for the Lord to save.

LAMENTATIONS 3:25–26

· · ·

Lord, every morning you hear my voice.
Every morning, I tell you what I need.
And I wait for your answer.

PSALM 5:3

God Needs Girls

God creates girls to fill important roles—
Both young and old, big and small.
Leaders, speakers, caretakers too—
God has a need for each and all!

Serving God brings you blessings in this life
and in the future life, too.

1 TIMOTHY 4:8

. . .

"I know what I have planned for you," says the Lord.
"I have good plans for you. I don't plan to hurt
you. I plan to give you hope and a good future."

JEREMIAH 29:11

. . .

You are young, but do not let anyone treat you as if
you were not important. Be an example to show the
believers how they should live. Show them with your
words, with the way you live, with your love, with your
faith, and with your pure life. Continue to read the
Scriptures to the people, strengthen them, and teach
them. Do these things until I come. . . . Then you will
save yourself and those people who listen to you.

1 TIMOTHY 4:12—13, 16

Using Your Gifts for God

Can you spike a volleyball across the net?
Or play beautiful songs on the guitar?
God has given YOU special gifts—
Now, go! Find out what they are!

Each of you received a spiritual gift. God has shown
you his grace in giving you different gifts. And you
are like servants who are responsible for using
God's gifts. So be good servants and use your
gifts to serve each other.

1 PETER 4:10

• • •

In all the work you are doing, work the best you can.
Work as if you were working for the Lord, not for
men. Remember that you will receive your reward
from the Lord, which he promised to his people.
You are serving the Lord Christ.

COLOSSIANS 3:23—24

We all have different gifts. Each gift came because
of the grace that God gave us.

ROMANS 12:6

• • •

There are different kinds of gifts; but they are all from the
same Spirit. There are different ways to serve; but all these
ways are from the same Lord. And there are different ways
that God works in people; but all these ways are from the
same God. God works in us all in everything we do.

1 CORINTHIANS 12:4–6

Making Each Day Count

Making the most of this life is how
You can thank the One who gives it.
Today is a day made just for you—
Now tell me, how will you live it?

Human life is like grass.
We grow like a flower in the field.
After the wind blows, the flower is gone.
There is no sign of where it was.
But the Lord's love for those who fear him
continues forever and ever.

PSALM 103:15—17

· · ·

Whoever spends time with wise people will become
wise. But whoever makes friends with fools will suffer.

PROVERBS 13:20

A person ought to enjoy every day of his life.
This is true no matter how long he lives. . . .
But remember that God will judge you
for everything you do.

ECCLESIASTES 11:8—9

Sharing Your Faith

Our faith is a wonderful gift from God,
A gift that He wants you to share.
At school, at play, at soccer, and ballet—
Share the Good News everywhere!

He said to them, "There are a great many people to harvest. But there are only a few workers to harvest them. God owns the harvest. Pray to God that he will send more workers to help gather his harvest."

LUKE 10:2

• • •

Let us look only to Jesus. He is the one who began our faith, and he makes our faith perfect.

HEBREWS 12:2

• • •

So go and make followers of all people in the world. . . . You can be sure that I will be with you always.

MATTHEW 28:19—20

• • •

Faith means being sure of the things we hope for. And faith means knowing that something is real even if we do not see it.

HEBREWS 11:1

He Is Your Savior

Jesus was born in a lowly manger;
He died and rose from death too. . . .
But the most amazing thing is this:
He chose to do it all for YOU.

He saved us because of his mercy, not because of good
deeds we did to be right with God. He saved us through the
washing that made us new people. He saved us by making us
new through the Holy Spirit. God poured out to us that
Holy Spirit fully through Jesus Christ our Savior.

TITUS 3:5–6

• • •

God makes people right with himself through their faith in
Jesus Christ. This is true for all who believe in Christ,
because all are the same. All people have sinned and are not
good enough for God's glory. People are made right with
God by his grace, which is a free gift. They are made right
with God by being made free from sin through Jesus Christ.

ROMANS 3:22–24

I tell you the truth. He who believes has eternal life.

JOHN 6:47

He Is Your Lord

Your Lord is the One you worship;
Your Lord is the One you obey.
Use your life to show others—
Jesus, your Lord, leads the way!

So God raised Christ to the highest place.
God made the name of Christ greater
than every other name.
God wants every knee to bow to Jesus—
everyone in heaven, on earth, and under the earth.
Everyone will say, "Jesus Christ is Lord"
and bring glory to God the Father.

PHILIPPIANS 2:9–11

. . .

If you declare with your mouth, "Jesus is Lord," and if
you believe in your heart that God raised Jesus from
death, then you will be saved.

ROMANS 10:9

. . .

God is strong and can help you not to fall. He can
bring you before his glory without any wrong in you
and give you great joy. He is the only God. He is the
One who saves us. To him be glory, greatness, power,
and authority through Jesus Christ our Lord for all
time past, now, and forever. Amen.

JUDE 24–25

He Is Your Friend

Always loving and forgiving,
A life with Him that will never end,
He's making a home for you in heaven—
Now that's what I call a Friend!

"Here I am! I stand at the door and knock. If anyone
hears my voice and opens the door, I will come in
and eat with him. And he will eat with me."

REVELATION 3:20

· · ·

Come near to God, and God will come near to you.
You are sinners. So clean sin out of your lives. You are
trying to follow God and the world at the same time.
Make your thinking pure.

JAMES 4:8

"This is my command: Love each other as
I have loved you. . . . You are my friends if you
do what I command you."

JOHN 15:12, 14

He Is Your Hope

His Word can never change;
His promises are forever true;
So put your hope in His words—
They were written just for you!

God uses my faith in Christ to make me right with
him. All I want is to know Christ and the power of
his rising from death. I want to share in Christ's
sufferings and become like him in his death.
If I have those things, then I have hope that
I myself will be raised from death.

PHILIPPIANS 3:9–11

• • •

So know that the Lord your God is God. He is the
faithful God. He will keep his agreement of love for
a thousand lifetimes. He does this for people
who love him and obey his commands.

DEUTERONOMY 7:9

• • •

Praise be to the God and Father of our Lord Jesus
Christ. God has great mercy, and because of his mercy
he gave us a new life. He gave us a living hope because
Jesus Christ rose from death. Now we hope for the
blessings God has for his children. These blessings are
kept for you in heaven. They cannot be destroyed
or be spoiled or lose their beauty.

1 PETER 1:3–4

He Is Your Example

Helpful, kind, and caring,
A humble servant too—
Jesus is your example;
His love can shine through you!

"If one of you wants to become great, then he must serve you like a servant. If one of you wants to become the most important, then he must serve all of you like a slave. In the same way, the Son of Man did not come to be served. He came to serve. The Son of Man came to give his life to save many people."

MARK 10:43–45

• • •

Let us look only to Jesus. He is the one who began our faith, and he makes our faith perfect. Jesus suffered death on the cross. But he accepted the shame of the cross as if it were nothing. He did this because of the joy that God put before him. And now he is sitting at the right side of God's throne.

HEBREWS 12:2

That is what you were called to do. Christ suffered
for you. He gave you an example to follow.
So you should do as he did. . . . And we are
healed because of his wounds.

1 PETER 2:21, 24

He Is Your Protector

Scary noises in the dark?
Afraid to make a peep?
Jesus is your Protector
He watches while you sleep.

You won't need to be afraid when you lie down.
When you lie down, your sleep will be peaceful.

PROVERBS 3:24

. • .

I go to bed and sleep in peace.
Lord, only you keep me safe.

PSALM 4:8

. • .

But the Lord is faithful. He will give you strength
and protect you from the Evil One.

2 THESSALONIANS 3:3

. • .

But I am close to God, and that is good.
The Lord God is my protection.
I will tell all that you have done.

PSALM 73:28

. • .

"The Lord your God is with you."

ZEPHANIAH 3:17

He Is Your Peace

When the stormy sea was raging
And His friends didn't know what to do,
Jesus calmed the storm for them,
And He can bring peace to you.

We have been made right with God because of our
faith. So we have peace with God through our Lord
Jesus Christ. Through our faith, Christ has brought us
into that blessing of God's grace that we now enjoy.
And we are happy because of the hope we have
of sharing God's glory.

ROMANS 5:1–2

· · ·

Let the peace that Christ gives control
your thinking. You were all called together in
one body to have peace. Always be thankful.

COLOSSIANS 3:15

The God who brings peace will soon defeat
Satan and give you power over him.
The grace of our Lord Jesus be with you.

ROMANS 16:20

He Is Your Joy

He offers love and peace
To every girl and boy—
Give your heart to Jesus,
And He will give you joy.

Your God has given you much joy.

. . .

[T]he Spirit gives love, joy, peace, patience, kindness, goodness, faithfulness, gentleness, self-control.

GALATIANS 5:22–23

. . .

Happy is the person who fears the Lord.
He loves what the Lord commands.

PSALM 112:1

The important things are living right with God, peace, and joy in the Holy Spirit. Anyone who serves Christ by living this way is pleasing God and will be accepted by other people.

ROMANS 14:17

God's Love Never Changes

God's love was, is, and will always be
As it's been throughout the ages—
It is perfect and lasts forever;
God's true love never changes.

God is love. Whoever lives in love lives in God,
and God lives in him.

1 JOHN 4:16

Yes, I am sure that nothing can separate us from the
love God has for us. Not death, not life, not angels,
not ruling spirits, nothing now, nothing in the future,
no powers, nothing above us, nothing below us,
or anything else in the whole world will ever be able
to separate us from the love of God that is in
Christ Jesus our Lord.

ROMANS 8:38—39

True love is God's love for us, not our love for God.
God sent his Son to die in our place to take away our
sins. That is how much God loved us, dear friends! So
we also must love each other. No one has ever seen
God. But if we love each other, God lives in us.

1 JOHN 4:10—12

God Will Help You Live for Him

The power to win against the world,
The strength to finish the race—
God promises these things to you,
When you accept His gift of grace.

"A thief comes to steal and kill and destroy. But I
came to give life—life in all its fullness."

JOHN 10:10

* * *

One man sinned, and so death ruled all people
because of that one man. But now some people accept
God's full grace and the great gift of being made right
with him. They will surely have true life and rule
through the one man, Jesus Christ.

ROMANS 5:17

* * *

Keeping your faith is like running a race. Try as hard
as you can to win. Be sure you receive the life that
continues forever. You were called to have that life.
And you confessed the great truth about Christ in a
way that many people heard.

1 TIMOTHY 6:12

God Is in Control

From the mountains to the valleys,
From the desert to the sea,
Our God controls it all, and still
He cares for *you* and *me*.

So God created human beings in his image. In the image of God he created them. He created them male and female. God blessed them and said, "Have many children and grow in number. Fill the earth and be its master. Rule over the fish in the sea and over the birds in the sky. Rule over every living thing that moves on the earth."

GENESIS 1:27–28

· · ·

Those who go to God Most High for safety will be protected by God All-Powerful.

PSALM 91:1

I will pray to the Lord.
And he will answer me from his holy mountain.
I can lie down and go to sleep.
And I will wake up again
because the Lord protects me.
Thousands of enemies may surround me.
But I am not afraid.

PSALM 3:4–6

God Will Answer Your Prayers

Just like a parent with a child
God wants to hear your every care;
He promises to answer you
When you take it to Him in prayer.

"And if you ask for anything in my name, I will do it for you. Then the Father's glory will be shown through the Son. If you ask me for anything in my name, I will do it."

JOHN 14:13–14

• • •

"Continue to ask, and God will give to you. Continue to search, and you will find. Continue to knock, and the door will open for you. Yes, everyone who continues asking will receive. He who continues searching will find. And he who continues knocking will have the door opened for him."

MATTHEW 7:7–8

• • •

"So I tell you to ask for things in prayer. And if you believe that you have received those things, then they will be yours."

MARK 11:24

• • •

"When you pray, you should go into your room and close the door. Then pray to your Father who cannot be seen. Your Father can see what is done in secret, and he will reward you."

MATTHEW 6:6

God Promises to Save You

Dear child, of all of God's promises,
It's the best one ever made:
When you believe in His Son, Jesus,
God promises you'll be saved.

"For God loved the world so much that he gave his only
Son. God gave his Son so that whoever believes in him
may not be lost, but have eternal life. God did not
send his Son into the world to judge the world guilty,
but to save the world through him."

JOHN 3:16—17

I mean that you have been saved by grace
because you believe. You did not save yourselves.
It was a gift from God.

EPHESIANS 2:8

Jesus said to her, "I am the resurrection and the life.
He who believes in me will have life even if he dies.
And he who lives and believes in me will never die."

JOHN 11:25–26

• • •

God will soon save those who respect him.
And his greatness will be seen in our land.

PSALM 85:9